STUDY GUIDE

The Origins and Course of the First World War, 1905–18

Edexcel - IGCSE

CLEVER Lili

Published by Clever Lili Limited.

contact@cleverlili.com

First published 2020

ISBN 978-1-913887-09-4

Copyright notice

All rights reserved. No part of this publication may be reproduced in any form or by any means (including photocopying or storing it in any medium by electronic means and whether or not transiently or incidentally to some other use of this publication) with the written permission of the copyright owner. Applications for the copyright owner's written permission should be addressed to the publisher.

Clever Lili has made every effort to contact copyright holders for permission for the use of copyright material. We will be happy, upon notification, to rectify any errors or omissions and include any appropriate rectifications in future editions.

Cover by: H. D. Girdwood / British Library on Unsplash

Icons by: flaticon and freepik

Contributors: Jordan Hobbis, James George, Hayleigh Snow, Bilal Ravat, Shahan Abu Shumel Haydar

Edited by Paul Connolly and Rebecca Parsley

Design by Evgeni Veskov and Will Fox

All rights reserved

DISCOVER MORE OF OUR IGCSE HISTORY STUDY GUIDES
GCSEHistory.com and Clever Lili

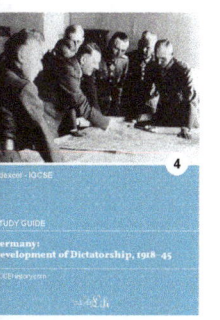

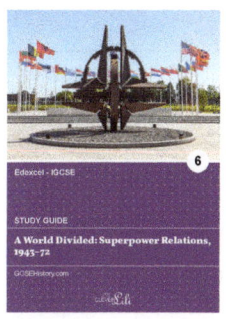

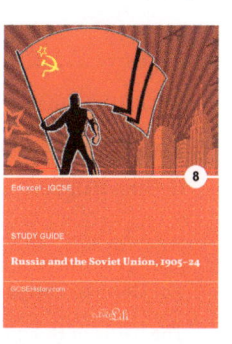

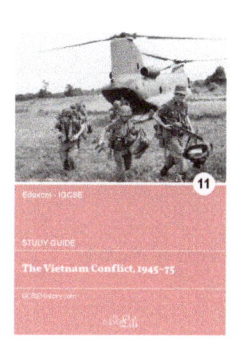

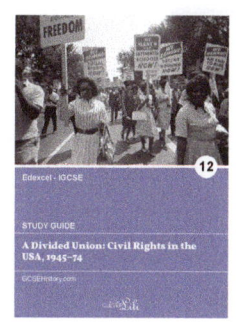

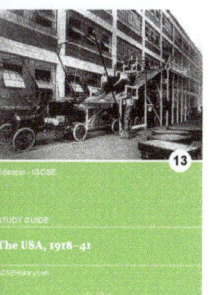

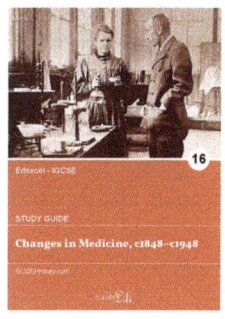

- 4 — Edexcel - IGCSE STUDY GUIDE — Germany: Development of Dictatorship, 1918-45
- 6 — Edexcel - IGCSE STUDY GUIDE — A World Divided: Superpower Relations, 1943-72
- 8 — Edexcel - IGCSE STUDY GUIDE — Russia and the Soviet Union, 1905-24
- 9 — Edexcel - IGCSE STUDY GUIDE — Dictatorship and Conflict in the USSR, 1924-53
- 11 — Edexcel - IGCSE STUDY GUIDE — The Vietnam Conflict, 1945-75
- 12 — Edexcel - IGCSE STUDY GUIDE — A Divided Union: Civil Rights in the USA, 1945-74
- 13 — Edexcel - IGCSE STUDY GUIDE — The USA, 1918-41
- 16 — Edexcel - IGCSE STUDY GUIDE — Changes in Medicine, c1848-c1948
- 40 — Edexcel - IGCSE STUDY GUIDE — China: Conflict, Crisis and Change, 1900-89

THE GUIDES ARE EVEN BETTER WITH OUR GCSE/IGCSE HISTORY WEBSITE APP AND MOBILE APP

GCSE History is a text and voice web and mobile app that allows you to easily revise for your GCSE/IGCSE exams wherever you are - it's like having your own personal GCSE history tutor. Whether you're at home or on the bus, GCSE History provides you with thousands of convenient bite-sized facts to help you pass your exams with flying colours. We cover all topics - with more than 120,000 questions - across the Edexcel,

Contents

How to use this book 5
What is this book about? 6
Revision suggestions 8

Timelines
Origins and Course of the First World War 12

International Rivalry
The First World War 14
Militarism 14
Alliances 15
Imperialism 15
Nationalism 16
Economic Rivalry 16
The Triple Alliance 17
The Triple Entente 18

The Growth of Tensions
The Naval Race 18
The First Moroccan Crisis 19
The Second Moroccan Crisis 20
The Bosnian Crisis 21
The First Balkan War 22
The Second Balkan War 22
The Black Hand 23
The Assassination of Archduke Franz Ferdinand 24

Deadlock on the Western Front
The July Days 25
The Schlieffen Plan 25
The Trench System 26
Deadlock on the Western Front 27
Life in the Trenches 28
Shell Shock 29
Trench foot 29
Trench fever 30
Dysentery 30
Gangrene 31
Treatment in the Trenches 31
New Weapons and Methods 32
Aircraft 32
Dogfights 33
Machine Guns 33
Poison Gas 34
Tanks 35

Artillery 35
The Battle of the Somme 36
The Battle of Passchendaele 37
General Haig 38

The War at Sea & Gallipoli
The German Threat in the North Sea 39
The Battle of Heligoland 39
German Raids 40
The Battle of Dogger Bank 41
The Battle of Jutland 41
Submarine Warfare 42
Anti U-Boat Measures 42
The Sinking of the Lusitania 43
The Gallipoli Campaign 44

Germany's Defeat
The Ludendorff Offensive 45
The USA and its Entry to the First World War 46
The Hundred Days Offensive 47
The End of the First World War 48

Glossary 50
Index 52

Quizzes, amazing exam preparation tools and more at GCSEHistory.com

HOW TO USE THIS BOOK

In this study guide, you will see a series of icons, highlighted words and page references. The key below will help you quickly establish what these mean and where to go for more information.

Icons

WHAT questions cover the key events and themes.

WHO questions cover the key people involved.

WHEN questions cover the timings of key events.

WHERE questions cover the locations of key moments.

WHY questions cover the reasons behind key events.

HOW questions take a closer look at the way in which events, situations and trends occur.

IMPORTANCE questions take a closer look at the significance of events, situations, and recurrent trends and themes.

DECISIONS questions take a closer look at choices made at events and situations during this era.

Highlighted words

Abdicate - occasionally, you will see certain words highlighted within an answer. This means that, if you need it, you'll find an explanation of the word or phrase in the glossary which starts on **page 50**.

Page references

Tudor *(p.7)* - occasionally, a certain subject within an answer is covered in more depth on a different page. If you'd like to learn more about it, you can go directly to the page indicated.

WHAT IS THIS BOOK ABOUT?

The Origins and Course of the First World War investigates why and how the world went to war in 1914. The course focuses on the causes and course of the First World War, examining 1905-1918. You will focus on crucial events during this period, and study the different political, economic and military changes that occurred.

Purpose
This study guide will help you to understand the complexities of the First World War. You will investigate themes such as militarism, nationalism, alliances and imperialism, while also exploring the role of economics, government and the military. This guide will enable you to develop the historical thinking skills of causation and consequence, similarity and difference, and change and continuity.

Topics
This study guide is split into five key areas.
- The Alliance System and International Rivalry.
- The Growth of Tension in Europe.
- The Schlieffen Plan and Deadlock on the Western Front.
- The War at Sea and Gallipoli.
- The Defeat of Germany.

Key Individuals
Some of the key individuals studied in this course include:
- Kaiser Wilhelm II.
- Archduke Franz Ferdinand.
- Winston Churchill.
- Alfred von Schlieffen.
- Sir Douglas Haig.
- Erich Ludendorff.

Key Events
Some of the key events and developments you will study on this course include:
- The formation of the alliance system.
- The Anglo-German naval race.
- International crises in the Balkans and Morocco.
- The assassination of Franz Ferdinand.
- The establishment of the Western Front in 1914.
- Trench conditions.
- The development of new weapons.
- Key battles on the Western Front: the Somme and Passchendaele.
- The war at sea.
- The Ludendorff Offensive.
- The Allied 100 days.
- German defeat and the armistice.

Assessment
Origins and Course of the First World War forms the first half of paper two. You will have a total of 1 hour and 30 minutes to complete the paper. You should spend 45 minutes on the First World War section of the paper. There will be 3 exam questions which will assess what you have learnt on the First World War course.
- Question 1 is worth 6 marks. This question will require you to describe TWO key features of a certain aspect of the First World War. For example, you could be asked to describe two key features of the Gallipoli campaign.

Quizzes, amazing exam preparation tools and more at GCSEHistory.com

WHAT IS THIS BOOK ABOUT?

- Question 2 is worth 8 marks. This question will require you to analyse two sources before explaining how far the sources support each other. It requires you to cross reference both sources, highlighting similarities AND differences, before concluding on the extent of support. You should aim to include three mini paragraphs explaining how the sources support each other, how they contradict each other before offering your own conclusion. For example, 'How far does Source A support the evidence of Source B about the threat posed.

- Question 3 is worth 16 marks. This question will give you a historical interpretation and you will then need to argue how far you agree or disagree with the statement on your chosen question. The focus of the question will always be different, focusing on one of the 2nd order concepts such as causation, consequence, change, continuity, similarity and difference. For this question you must use the interpretation alongside the sources from question 2. For example, 'Extract C suggests that Germany was mainly responsible for the outbreak of the First World War. How far do you agree with this interpretation?'.

REVISION SUGGESTIONS

Revision! A dreaded word. Everyone knows it's coming, everyone knows how much it helps with your exam performance, and everyone struggles to get started! We know you want to do the best you can in your IGCSEs, but schools aren't always clear on the best way to revise. This can leave students wondering:

- ✓ How should I plan my revision time?
- ✓ How can I beat procrastination?
- ✓ What methods should I use? Flash cards? Re-reading my notes? Highlighting?

Luckily, you no longer need to guess at the answers. Education researchers have looked at all the available revision studies, and the jury is in. They've come up with some key pointers on the best ways to revise, as well as some thoughts on popular revision methods that aren't so helpful. The next few pages will help you understand what we know about the best revision methods.

How can I beat procrastination?

This is an age-old question, and it applies to adults as well! Have a look at our top three tips below.

Reward yourself

When we think a task we have to do is going to be boring, hard or uncomfortable, we often put if off and do something more 'fun' instead. But we often don't really enjoy the 'fun' activity because we feel guilty about avoiding what we should be doing. Instead, get your work done and promise yourself a reward after you complete it. Whatever treat you choose will seem all the sweeter, and you'll feel proud for doing something you found difficult. Just do it!

Just do it!

We tend to procrastinate when we think the task we have to do is going to be difficult or dull. The funny thing is, the most uncomfortable part is usually making ourselves sit down and start it in the first place. Once you begin, it's usually not nearly as bad as you anticipated.

Pomodoro technique

The pomodoro technique helps you trick your brain by telling it you only have to focus for a short time. Set a timer for 20 minutes and focus that whole period on your revision. Turn off your phone, clear your desk, and work. At the end of the 20 minutes, you get to take a break for five. Then, do another 20 minutes. You'll usually find your rhythm and it becomes easier to carry on because it's only for a short, defined chunk of time.

Spaced practice

We tend to arrange our revision into big blocks. For example, you might tell yourself: "This week I'll do all my revision for the Cold War, then next week I'll do the Medicine Through Time unit."

REVISION SUGGESTIONS

This is called **massed practice**, because all revision for a single topic is done as one big mass.

But there's a better way! Try **spaced practice** instead. Instead of putting all revision sessions for one topic into a single block, space them out. See the example below for how it works.

This means planning ahead, rather than leaving revision to the last minute - but the evidence strongly suggests it's worth it. You'll remember much more from your revision if you use **spaced practice** rather than organising it into big blocks. Whichever method you choose, though, remember to reward yourself with breaks.

Spaced practice (more effective):

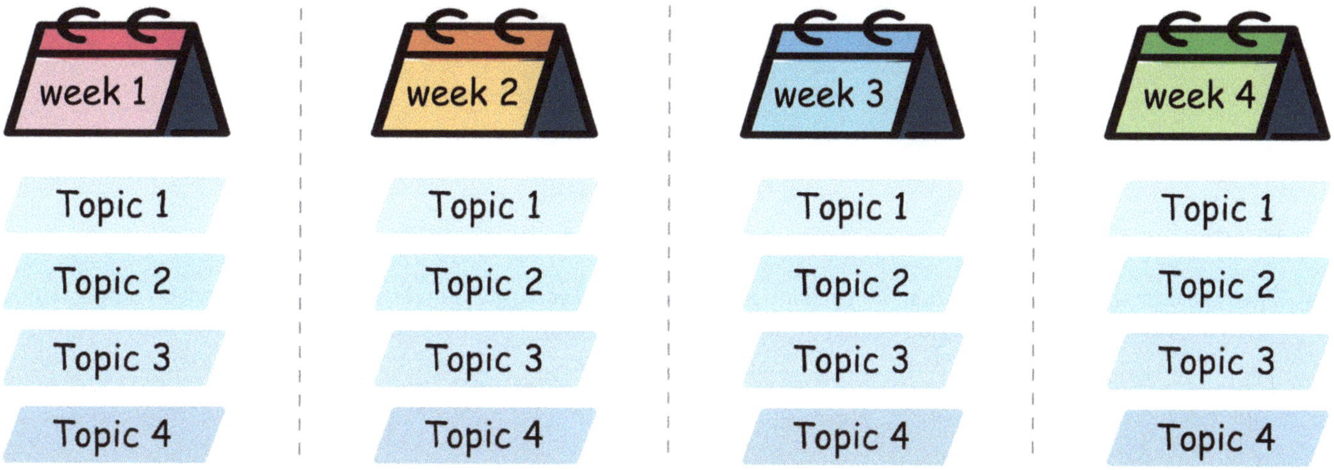

week 1	week 2	week 3	week 4
Topic 1	Topic 1	Topic 1	Topic 1
Topic 2	Topic 2	Topic 2	Topic 2
Topic 3	Topic 3	Topic 3	Topic 3
Topic 4	Topic 4	Topic 4	Topic 4

Massed practice (less effective)

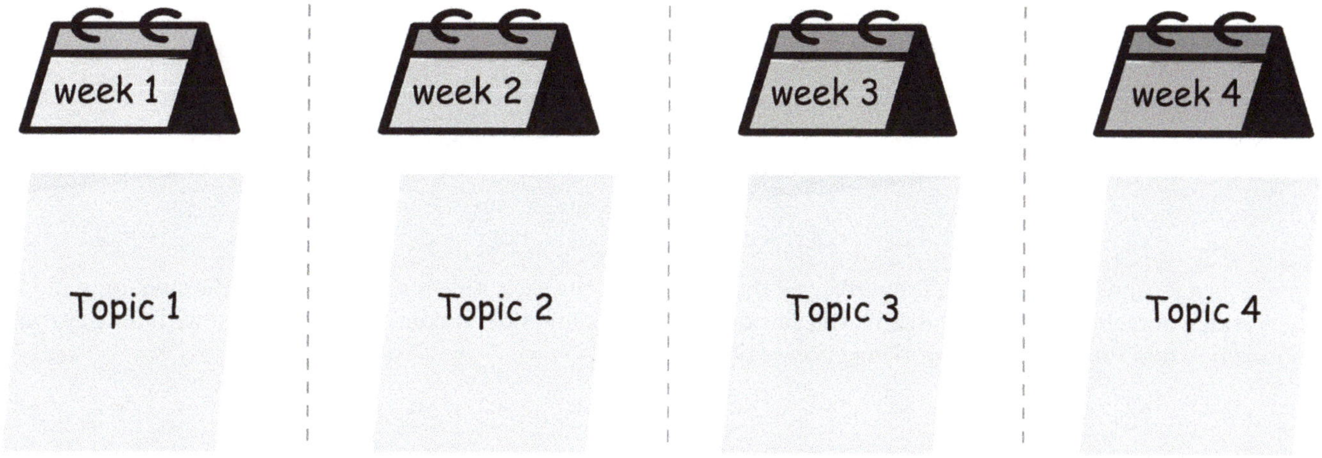

week 1	week 2	week 3	week 4
Topic 1	Topic 2	Topic 3	Topic 4

REVISION SUGGESTIONS

What methods should I use to revise?

Self-testing/flash cards

Self explanation/mind-mapping

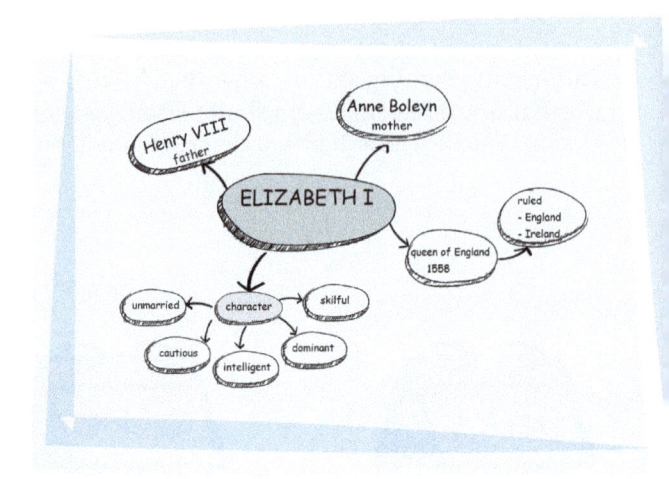

The research shows a clear winner for revision methods - **self-testing**. A good way to do this is with **flash cards.** Flash cards are really useful for helping you recall short – but important – pieces of information, like names and dates.

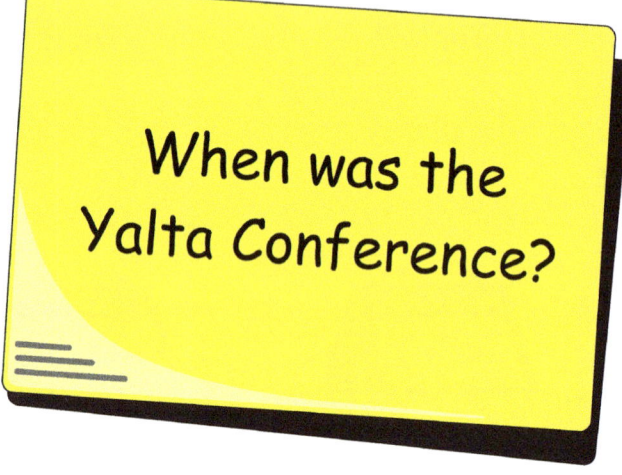

Side A - question

Side B - answer

Write questions on one side of the cards, and the answers on the back. This makes answering the questions and then testing yourself easy. Put all the cards you get right in a pile to one side, and only repeat the test with the ones you got wrong - this will force you to work on your weaker areas.

pile with right answers

pile with wrong answers

As this book has a quiz question structure itself, you can use it for this technique.

Another good revision method is **self-explanation**. This is where you explain how and why one piece of information from your course linked with another piece.

This can be done with **mind-maps**, where you draw the links and then write explanations for how they connect. For example, President Truman is connected with anti-communism because of the Truman Doctrine.

Quizzes, amazing exam preparation tools and more at GCSEHistory.com

REVISION SUGGESTIONS

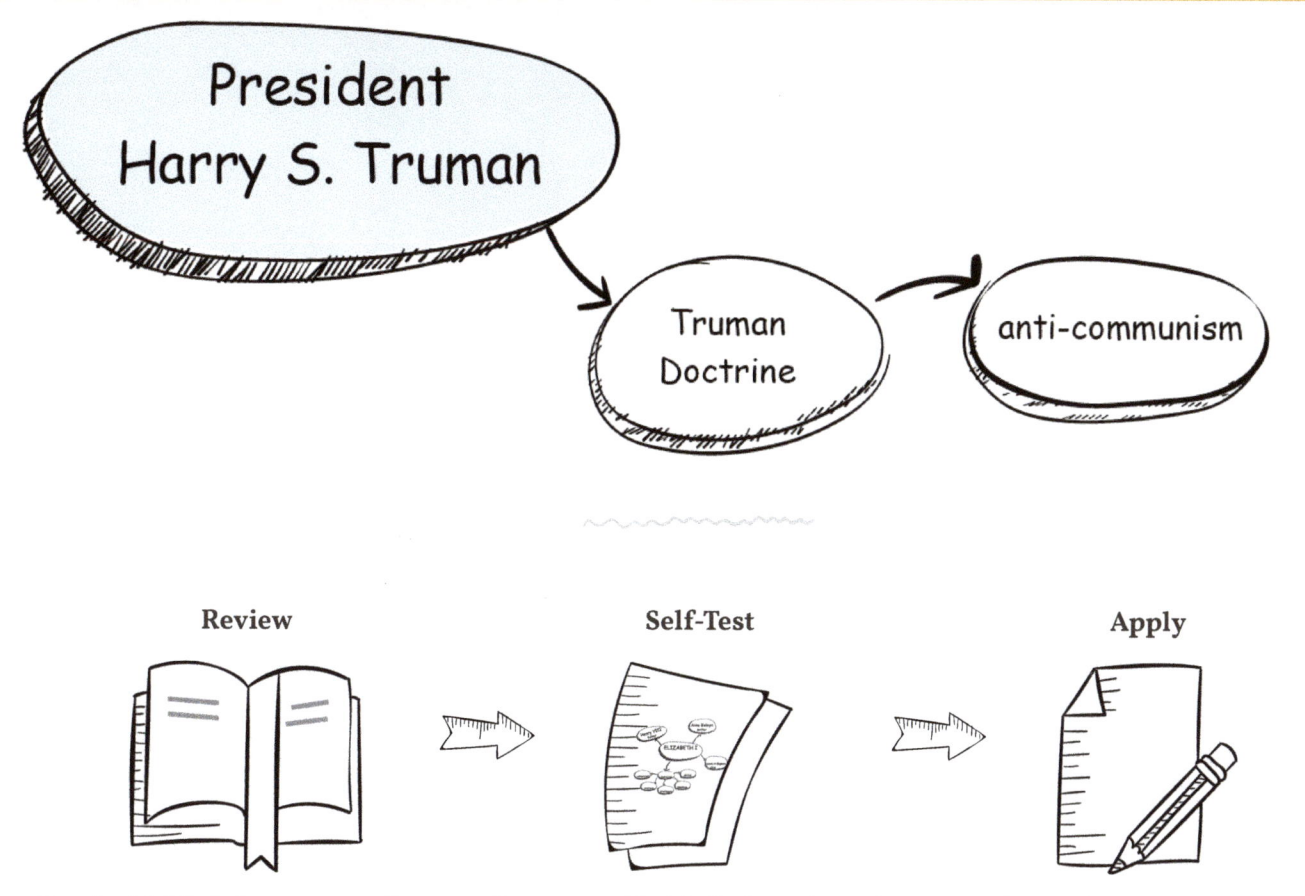

President Harry S. Truman → Truman Doctrine → anti-communism

Review

Start by highlighting or re-reading to create your flashcards for self-testing.

Self-Test

Test yourself with flash cards. Make mind maps to explain the concepts.

Apply

Apply your knowledge on practice exam questions.

Which revision techniques should I be cautious about?

Highlighting and **re-reading** are not necessarily bad strategies - but the research does say they're less effective than flash cards and mind-maps.

Highlighting

Re-reading

If you do use these methods, make sure they are **the first step to creating flash cards**. Really engage with the material as you go, rather than switching to autopilot.

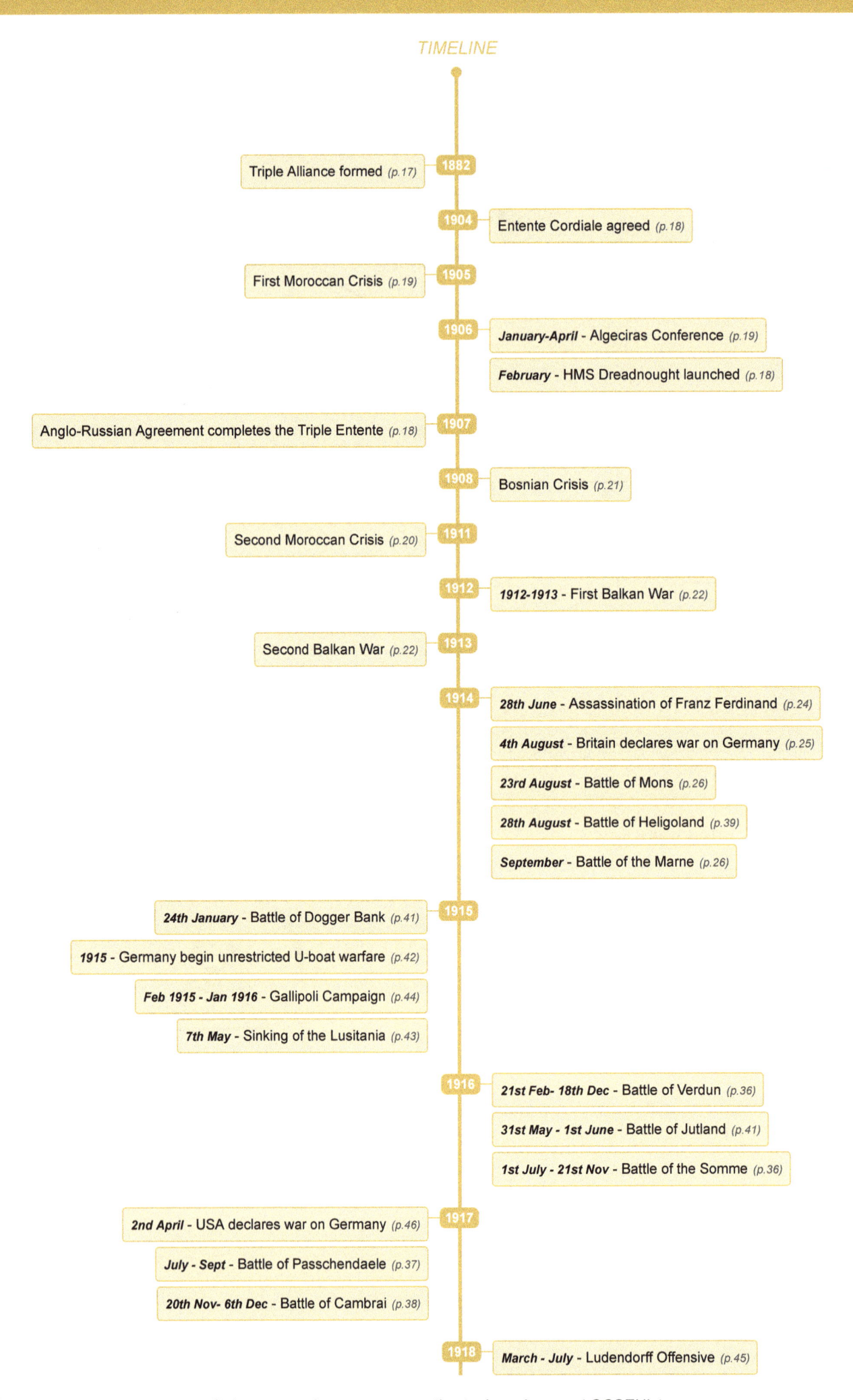

ORIGINS AND COURSE OF THE FIRST WORLD WAR

TIMELINE

- **1882** — Triple Alliance formed *(p.17)*
- **1904** — Entente Cordiale agreed *(p.18)*
- **1905** — First Moroccan Crisis *(p.19)*
- **1906**
  - *January-April* - Algeciras Conference *(p.19)*
  - *February* - HMS Dreadnought launched *(p.18)*
- **1907** — Anglo-Russian Agreement completes the Triple Entente *(p.18)*
- **1908** — Bosnian Crisis *(p.21)*
- **1911** — Second Moroccan Crisis *(p.20)*
- **1912** — *1912-1913* - First Balkan War *(p.22)*
- **1913** — Second Balkan War *(p.22)*
- **1914**
  - *28th June* - Assassination of Franz Ferdinand *(p.24)*
  - *4th August* - Britain declares war on Germany *(p.25)*
  - *23rd August* - Battle of Mons *(p.26)*
  - *28th August* - Battle of Heligoland *(p.39)*
  - *September* - Battle of the Marne *(p.26)*
- **1915**
  - *24th January* - Battle of Dogger Bank *(p.41)*
  - *1915* - Germany begin unrestricted U-boat warfare *(p.42)*
  - *Feb 1915 - Jan 1916* - Gallipoli Campaign *(p.44)*
  - *7th May* - Sinking of the Lusitania *(p.43)*
- **1916**
  - *21st Feb - 18th Dec* - Battle of Verdun *(p.36)*
  - *31st May - 1st June* - Battle of Jutland *(p.41)*
  - *1st July - 21st Nov* - Battle of the Somme *(p.36)*
- **1917**
  - *2nd April* - USA declares war on Germany *(p.46)*
  - *July - Sept* - Battle of Passchendaele *(p.37)*
  - *20th Nov - 6th Dec* - Battle of Cambrai *(p.38)*
- **1918** — *March - July* - Ludendorff Offensive *(p.45)*

Quizzes, amazing exam preparation tools and more at GCSEHistory.com

ORIGINS AND COURSE OF THE FIRST WORLD WAR

8th Aug - 11th Nov - Allied 100 Days Offensive *(p.47)*

October - German navy mutinies

9th Nov - Kaiser Wilhelm II abdicates *(p.48)*

11th Nov - Armistice signed *(p.48)*

THE FIRST WORLD WAR

The First World War would become the largest and most widespread conflict in history up to that point. However, it also inspired great advancements in science and technology.

What was the First World War?

The First World War (also known as the Great War) was a global conflict that lasted from 1914-1918.

Who was on each side in the First World War?

The war was fought between the Central Powers (Germany, Austria-Hungary, Bulgaria, and the Ottoman Empire) and the Allied Powers (France, Russia, Belgium, Serbia, and Britain). The Allies were later joined by the USA and Italy.

When did the First World War take place?

The First World War started on July 28th 1914, and ended on 11th November 1918.

Where did the First World War happen?

The First World War took place across the world, both on land and at sea. Most of the fighting occurred in Europe and Russia, although there were smaller battles in the Middle East, Africa and China.

Why did the First World War happen?

The war broke out due to a number of short and long term reasons, which can be summarised as follows:

- Militarism *(p.14)*.
- Alliances.
- Imperialism. *(p.15)*
- Nationalism *(p.16)*.
- Economic rivalry *(p.16)*.

DID YOU KNOW?

The war had a different name at the time!
It was known as the 'Great War'. Some even referred to it as the 'European War' due to the majority of participants and fighting taking place in Europe.

MILITARISM

Strong armed forces were important to maintain and challenge Great Power status. These led to an arms race between countries as they tried to get the upper hand on their rivals.

What is militarism?

Militarism is the idea that a country should have a strong military and be prepared to use it.

How did militarism lead to the First World War?

Due to the alliance system, countries grew afraid of being surrounded by hostile states. As a consequence, they increased the size of their armies and navies, which created more fear and led to an arms race.

> **DID YOU KNOW?**
>
> **Many countries overestimated the strength of their armed forces.**
> In Britain, many observers believed that the war would be over by Christmas due to their military strength.

ALLIANCES

Alliances between countries were littered across Europe and the world as powers scrambled to find allies. With alliances, came combined strength and a great chance of success.

What were the alliances in the First World War?

There were two pre-First World War alliances. The Triple Entente *(p.18)* consisted of Britain, Russia and France. The Triple Alliance *(p.17)* was formed by Germany, Austria-Hungary and Italy.

How did alliances lead to the First World War?

In order to achieve security, countries often formed alliances to protect themselves. Tensions between alliances meant that, when Austria-Hungary declared war on Serbia in 1914, others felt obligated to join the conflict.

> **DID YOU KNOW?**
>
> **Family loyalties were soon tested!**
> George V (England) and Wilhelm II (Germany) were actually first cousins! However, the family ties didn't stop there. George and Tsar Nicholas II were also first cousins and joined forces in the Triple Entente.

IMPERIALISM

'Should the worst happen...Australians will stand beside the mother country to help and defend her to our last man and our last shilling.' Andrew Fisher, 1914.

What is imperialism?

Imperialism is the desire to acquire colonies and create an empire.

How did imperialism lead to the First World War?

Germany attempted to challenge the large overseas empires already held by France and Britain. This was an issue as colonies provided raw materials, and were markets for goods produced by the European powers that governed them. If they lost these, they lost money.

Who were the countries which followed a policy of imperialism?

- Great Britain had 56 colonies, with a total population of 390 million.
- France had 29 colonies, with a total population of 58 million.
- Russia had 0 colonies, although it was looking to expand in the Balkans.
- Germany had 10 colonies, with a total population of 15 million.
- Austria-Hungary had 0 colonies, although it did control other European countries such as Bosnia.

> **DID YOU KNOW?**
>
> **Britain had a vast empire by the start of the First World War.**
>
> The British Empire stretched across the world with countries such as Canada and Australia, along with a number of countries within Africa, Asia and the Middle East. This included around 412 million people and 23% of the world's population.

NATIONALISM

'I think a curse should rest on me — because I love this war. I know it's...shattering the lives of thousands — and yet — I can't help it — I enjoy every second of it.' Winston Churchill, 1916.

What is nationalism?

Nationalism is having strong support for your own country's independence and interests. This may lead to people believing their country is superior to others.

How did nationalism lead to the First World War?

When nationalism is too strong, it can lead to competition between countries. This inspired many people to support war and join up to fight in 1914. This is closely linked to imperialism *(p.15)* as it promotes the idea of one 'superior' country ruling over others.

> **DID YOU KNOW?**
>
> **Germany wanted to unite all Germanic-speaking people under one country.**
>
> Pan-Germanism (Pangermanismus in German) was the nationalist idea that helped to motivate Germany's entry into the First World War. It was particularly interested in the lands east of Germany.

ECONOMIC RIVALRY

Money was a driving force for the start of the First World War. The more money a country had, the more powerful it could become.

What is economic rivalry?

Economic rivalry is the tension created from competing with others to gain wealth for your country.

How did economic rivalry lead to the First World War?
Economic rivalry is the competition between countries to gain more wealth. It created tension between the alliances in the years before 1914.

> **DID YOU KNOW?**
>
> **War needed money but war also created money for the winners!**
>
> The prizes for winning a war could be huge! Britain's and America's GDP grew 20% even during the war. However for France, where the majority of fighting took place, their GDP shrunk by 40%!

THE TRIPLE ALLIANCE

'We see the European Great Powers divided into two great camps. On the one side Germany, Austria, and Italy have concluded a defensive alliance, whose sole object is to guard against hostile aggression' General Friedrich von Bernhardi, 1914.

What was the Triple Alliance?
The Triple Alliance was an agreement between Germany, Austria-Hungary and Italy, to provide military support to each other.

When was the Triple Alliance created?
The Triple Alliance was formed in May 1882.

Who was in the Triple Alliance?
The Triple Alliance consisted of three of Europe's great powers in 1914: Germany, Austria-Hungary and Italy.

Why was the Triple Alliance formed?
The Triple Alliance provided mutual support for the smaller countries; it was a chance to have a more powerful ally. For Germany, the alliance provided protection against encirclement by France and Russia.

> **DID YOU KNOW?**
>
> **Three's a crowd....well not in this case.**
>
> The Triple Alliance was originally called the Dual Alliance when agreed in 1879. When Italy joined in 1882, it became the Triple Alliance.

THE TRIPLE ENTENTE

The second of two 'camps' of the European powers. Later to form but equally as powerful, the rifts in European relations were now cemented.

What was the Triple Entente?
The Triple Entente was a military coalition between the Great Britain, France and Russia against any potential enemies.

When was the Triple Entente created?
The Triple Entente was created in 1907 when Russia joined Britain, who had previously united in the Entente Cordiale in 1904.

Who were members of the Triple Entente?
The Triple Entente consisted of three of Europe's great powers in 1914 - Russia, France and Great Britain.

Why was the Triple Entente formed?
The purpose of the Triple Entente was to protect its members against the growing threat of Germany and to support each other if there was a war.

DID YOU KNOW?

All for one and one for all!

The Triple Entente was underpinned by a series of agreements which unified the Allies. For example, it was agreed that no individual country could seek separate peace deals.

THE NAVAL RACE

Britain begins to consolidate and expand its domination of the seas. It had the least to gain but the most to lose!

What was the naval race?
The naval race was a competition between Germany and Britain to have naval supremacy. The race was 'run' between 1906 and 1914.

Why did Germany want to challenge the British navy and start the naval race?
Britain relied on its navy to keep sea routes open to its empire and protect its economic interests. Germany wanted to become a world power, and Britain saw this as a threat to its own empire.

What ships were the focus of the naval race?
In 1906 Britain launched a new battleship, HMS Dreadnought. It was the most advanced warship of the time: faster, more heavily armoured and with bigger guns than previous warships. Germany built its own dreadnoughts, which led to a naval arms race between the two countries.

Who won the naval race?

Between 1906 and 1914 Britain built 29 dreadnoughts, compared with Germany's 17.

> **DID YOU KNOW?**
>
> **The Germans didn't have much confidence in their older ships.**
> During the naval race, Germans called their older ships 'funf minuten' because they wouldn't last five minutes against a dreadnought.

THE FIRST MOROCCAN CRISIS

'On the whole the brief visit of His Majesty came off splendidly...and apparently made a great impression upon both Moroccans and foreigners.' Councillor von Schoen, 1905.

What was the First Moroccan Crisis?

The First Moroccan Crisis was a political dispute between France and Germany, after France declared its intention to have control (a mandate) over Morocco.

Which countries were involved in the First Moroccan Crisis?

France and Germany were the main countries involved. France had agreed with other European powers that it would take control of Morocco, but Germany hadn't been consulted.

Where was the First Moroccan Crisis?

The crisis was over Morocco, one of the few independent African states not colonised by a European power.

When was the First Moroccan Crisis?

The dispute took place from March 1905, and was solved with the Algeciras Conference in April 1906.

Why did the First Moroccan Crisis happen?

The crisis emerged due to the Kaiser's desire to promote Germany's strength as part of his weltpolitik strategy, and to test the Entente Cordiale.

What was the German reaction to the First Moroccan Crisis?

When Germany heard about France's plan to control Morocco, Kaiser Wilhelm II visited Tangier in Morocco to show his support for Morocco's independence. He didn't want France to become too powerful.

What was the French reaction to the First Moroccan Crisis?

France was shocked by Germany's position. The French press and politicians reacted angrily, as they believed it was a simple matter and Germany should not interfere, given the country's limited number of colonies.

What were the consequences of the First Moroccan Crisis?

There were 3 outcomes from the First Moroccan Crisis:

- It strengthened the Entente Cordiale and led to the Anglo-Russian Agreement of 1907, therefore completing the Triple Entente *(p. 18)*.
- It angered the German Kaiser greatly. He felt embarrassed, and would not back down in any further dispute. This attitude would eventually lead to the Second Moroccan Crisis *(p. 20)*.

DID YOU KNOW?

Kaiser Wilhelm II was furious following the First Moroccan Crisis and demanded revenge.

He exclaimed 'Paris must get one in the eye from us one day!'

THE SECOND MOROCCAN CRISIS

'What the French contemplate doing is not wise, but we cannot under our agreement interfere'. Sir Edward Grey, 1911.

What was the Second Moroccan Crisis?

The Second Moroccan Crisis was a political dispute between France and Germany, when Morocco appealed for help from France and Spain after rebels rose against the sultan.

Which countries were involved in the Second Moroccan Crisis?

France, Germany and Spain were the main countries involved. France and Spain both sent troops to Fez in May 1911 to help support the sultan. In response, Germany sent a gunboat, SMS Panther, to the port of Agadir.

Where was the Second Moroccan Crisis?

The crisis was focused on Fez, a city in the north of Morocco, but it also stretched to the port of Agadir where the Germans sent their gunboat.

When was the Second Moroccan Crisis?

The dispute began in March 1911 and was resolved with the Treaty of Fez in November 1911.

How did Germany react to the Second Moroccan Crisis?

When Germany heard about France's involvement, they believed the French were using this as a way to occupy Morocco. Germany sent a warship to Morocco, as France's actions went against the Treaty of Algeciras.

How did France react to the Second Moroccan Crisis?

The French reacted to Germany's warship by sending more troops to Morocco. Britain tried to persuade France against doing this, but concern about the behaviour of Germany meant they had to support the action.

How did the Second Moroccan Crisis end?

It ended as Germany was hit by a financial crisis and couldn't deal with both events at the same time. The Germans withdrew their warship and left Morocco.

What were the consequences of the Second Moroccan Crisis?

There were 5 key outcomes from the Second Moroccan Crisis:

- The Treaty of Fez was signed between France and Germany, which agreed that France could take control of Morocco. In return, the French would give parts of the Congo to Germany.
- Tensions between France, Britain and Germany reached breaking point. This event showed the lengths all countries would go to in order to defend their interests.
- British support for France during the crisis strengthened the Entente Cordiale.
- The division between the Entente powers and Germany continued to increase.
- It weakened the Triple Alliance *(p.17)*, as Italy did not support Germany in the crisis.

> **DID YOU KNOW?**
>
> **Tensions were already beginning to flare in 1911!**
> David Lloyd George issued a warning to Germany to offer fair terms to France, stating that 'peace at that price (British disadvantage) would be a humiliation intolerable for a great country like ours to endure'.

THE BOSNIAN CRISIS

Tensions start to come to the boil with annexation of the Balkan provinces of Bosnia and Herzegovina by by Austria-Hungary.

What was the Bosnian Crisis?

While the 1908 Turkish Revolution was taking place, Austria annexed Bosnia and Herzegovina, which had been under Turkish control. However, the king of Serbia claimed Bosnia & Herzegovina should belong to his country.

What were the consequences of the Bosnian Crisis?

There were 5 main outcomes from the Bosnian Crisis:

- It increased tension between the alliances, as Russia stepped in to support Serbia, while Germany took Austria-Hungary's side.
- The Balkan League, consisting of Bulgaria, Greece, Montenegro and Serbia, was set up with the goal of forcing Turkey out of Europe.
- Russia backed down and began to rearm.
- Austria-Hungary now felt it could rely on support from Germany in the future.
- It weakened the Triple Alliance *(p.17)*, as Italy refused to support Austria-Hungary.

> **DID YOU KNOW?**
>
> **There was a cover up attempt by Austria-Hungary to justify their actions in Bosnia.**
> Known as the Agram Trial, Austria-Hungary sentenced 31 Serbs for their role in trying to overthrow the state. However, it was later found that one of the Austrian-Hungarian ministers had forged the documents. The 31 Serbs were then released.

THE FIRST BALKAN WAR

The Balkan League united to defeat the troubled and declining Ottoman Empire. The Ottoman's foothold in Europe was devastated.

What was the First Balkan War?
The First Balkan War was a war between Turkey and the Balkan League.

When was the First Balkan War?
The war took place from October 1912 to May 1913.

What countries were involved in the First Balkan War?
Turkey fought against the four members of the Balkan League - Bulgaria, Greece, Montenegro and Serbia.

What happened in the First Balkan War?
The Turkish were overpowered by the Balkan forces, and surrendered after just 50 days of actual fighting.

What were the consequences of the First Balkan War?
Turkey gave up its land in Europe and this was divided between the Balkan states.

DID YOU KNOW?

Turkey was known as the 'sick man of Europe' at this time!
Turkey was known as this due to the decline of the once-feared Ottoman Empire.

THE SECOND BALKAN WAR

As newly 'liberated' states scrambled to establish themselves, Bulgaria aired their disagreement with the outcome of the First Balkan War. The failure to agree would bring the region to war again.

What was the Second Balkan War?
The Second Balkan War was fought between Bulgaria, Serbia and Greece. Serbia and Greece supported each other and were backed by Turkey and Romania.

What caused the Second Balkan War?
Bulgaria was not happy with the way in which Turkey's land had been divided up among the Balkan League countries.

When was the Second Balkan War?
The war started in June 1913, a month after the original peace agreement from the first war. Bulgaria was soon overpowered, and an armistice was signed in August 1913.

What countries were involved in the Second Balkan War?
Bulgaria fought against Greece, Serbia, Turkey and Romania.

What happened in the Second Balkan War?

Bulgaria invaded Greece and Serbia in June. However, Bulgaria did not expect the unified response from the other countries and was forced to ask for an armistice.

What were the consequences of the Second Balkan War?

There were 5 key outcomes from the Second Balkan War:
- ☑ Serbia gained territory and grew more aggressive towards other Balkan countries following its success.
- ☑ Serbians in Bosnia-Herzegovina were inspired by the victory and wanted to join Serbia.
- ☑ Austria-Hungary became concerned by the possibility of revolt within its empire, specifically in Bosnia.
- ☑ Austria-Hungary was committed to trying to control Serbia.
- ☑ Bulgaria was resentful of Serbia's gain and was waiting for an opportunity to gain back some of its lost land.

> **DID YOU KNOW?**
>
> **People began to consider and research the impact of war on civilian populations.**
>
> The Carnegie Endowment for International Peace produced one of the first internationally read reports on civilians during war.

THE BLACK HAND

A secret organisation founded by Dragutin Dimitrijević to promote unification of the South Slavic majority under Serbia or Montenegro.

What was the Black Hand?

The Black Hand was a secret society which aimed to unite all Serbs who were ruled by either the Ottoman Empire or Austria-Hungary.

Who was involved in the Black Hand?

The Black Hand was founded by ten Serbian army officers, led by Colonel Dragutin Dimitrijević. However, membership soon grew to more than 2,500 members.

When did the Black Hand form?

The Black Hand was formed on 22nd May, 1911.

Why was the Black Hand formed?

Slavic nationalism *(p.16)* had grown following the Bosnian crisis *(p.21)*, and there was now a desire to unite all Slavs in a Greater Serbia.

What methods did the Black Hand use?

The Black Hand planted bombs, and carried out assassinations and general acts of sabotage in foreign countries which controlled a Serbian population.

Why was the Black Hand important?

The Black Hand would later assassinate Archduke Franz Ferdinand *(p.24)*, heir to the Austrian throne, and spark the beginning of the First World War.

> **DID YOU KNOW?**
>
> **The Black Hand had another name.**
> It was also known as 'Ujedinjenje Ili smrt', which translates to 'Union or death'.

THE ASSASSINATION OF ARCHDUKE FRANZ FERDINAND

'I come to Sarajevo on a visit, and I get bombs thrown at me. It is outrageous!' Archduke Franz Ferdinand following the first assassination attempt, 1914.

What happened to Archduke Franz Ferdinand?

Archduke Franz Ferdinand, the heir to the Austro-Hungarian throne, was shot and fatally wounded.

Who killed Archduke Franz Ferdinand?

Gavrilo Princip, a member of the Black Hand *(p.23)*, assassinated the archduke using a revolver.

Where was Archduke Franz Ferdinand assassinated?

Archduke Franz Ferdinand was assassinated in Sarajevo, the capital of Bosnia.

When was the assassination of Archduke Franz Ferdinand?

The assassination was carried out on 28th June, 1914.

Why was Archduke Franz Ferdinand assassinated?

Archduke Franz Ferdinand was assassinated by the Black Hand *(p.23)* in an attempt to make sure he didn't pacify the Serbians in Bosnia. Pacifying the Serbians in Bosnia would strengthen the archduke's position when he came to the throne but would also undermine Serbia's plans to unite all Slavs in a Greater Serbia - the Black Hand wanted an independent Serbia, free from Austro-Hungarian and Ottoman rule.

What were the consequences of the assassination of Archduke Franz Ferdinand?

The main outcome of the assassination was the outbreak of the First World War. This happened in the aftermath of the assassination, during the 'July Days'.

> **DID YOU KNOW?**
>
> **All the assassins were caught and tried for their crime.**
> Gavrilo Princip, the assassin, was too young to receive the death sentence. He died in prison of tuberculosis in 1918.

THE JULY DAYS

'The lamps are going out all over Europe. We shall not see them lit again in our lifetime' Sir Edward Grey, August 1914.

What were the 'July Days' before the outbreak of the First World War?
The July Days is the name given to the period between the assassination of Archduke Franz Ferdinand *(p.24)* and the start of the First World War.

What were the key events of the First World War 'July Days'?
The July Days are made up of 10 key exchanges between alliances;
- 28th June, 1914: Assassination of Franz Ferdinand.
- 5th July, 1914: Germany agreed to support Austria-Hungary in a potential conflict with Serbia. This is known as the 'blank cheque'.
- 23rd July, 1914: Austria-Hungary sent an ultimatum to Serbia.
- 25th July, 1914: Serbia agreed to all of Austria's demands except one.
- 26th July, 1914: Russia promised to support Serbia in any conflict.
- 28th July, 1914: Austria-Hungary declared war on Serbia. Serbia requested the support of Russia.
- 29th July, 1914: Germany warned Russia not to get involved but Russia mobilised its army. Two days later, Germany also warned France not to intervene.
- 1st August, 1914: Germany declared war on Russia and, in return, France mobilised its army.
- 2nd August, 1914: Germany requested access to Belgium, to attack France as part of the Schlieffen Plan *(p.25)*. Belgium refused. A day later, Germany declared war on France and invaded Belgium.
- 4th August, 1914: Britain declared war on Germany.

DID YOU KNOW?

War was not inevitable.
The German ambassador in Austria-Hungary wrote to Berlin of his attempts to calm the situation; 'I take opportunity of every such occasion to advise quietly but very impressively and seriously against too hasty steps'.

THE SCHLIEFFEN PLAN

With the war begun, the Germans aim to strike hard and quickly across Europe. However, this one, inflexible, plan of attack in the west quickly began to go wrong.

What was the Schlieffen Plan?
The Schlieffen Plan was a German war plan to avoid a war on two fronts by attacking France, travelling at high speed through Belgium. After defeating France, the German Army would then east turn and attack Russia.

When was the Schlieffen Plan created?
The plan was created in December 1905, though it was not employed until August 1914.

Who created the Schlieffen Plan?

The Schlieffen Plan was created by the most senior general in the German Army, Count Alfred von Schlieffen.

Why was the Schlieffen Plan created?

The plan was created in preparation for war due to growing rivalries at the time. Germany was particularly worried about being encircled by France and Russia.

Why did the Schlieffen Plan fail?

The Schlieffen Plan failed for 6 key reasons:

- The Germans could not keep to the 6-week timetable for defeating France: the Belgian Army slowed the German advance at forts around Liege, while the BEF slowed it further at the Battle of Mons.
- The use of Plan 17, which was the French war plan to attack Germany's industrial centre, slowed the German advance by two weeks. However, the plan proved an overall failure for the French.
- Russian mobilisation came more quickly than expected and Russia invaded eastern Germany on 19th August. This caused Germany to send 100,000 troops to the east, weakening its attack against France.
- German supplies of food and ammunition could not keep up with the rapid advance, leaving soldiers tired, hungry and under-equipped.
- General von Kluck changed the plan. Instead of encircling Paris he decided to meet the French and British head on and aim to win a decisive victory at the Battle of the Marne, but was defeated.
- At the Battle of the Marne the Germans were forced back to the River Aisne where they began to dig trenches.

What were the consequences of the failure of the Schlieffen Plan?

The failure of the Schlieffen Plan had 2 important consequences:

- It meant the Germans would now have to fight a war on two fronts, reducing their chance of victory.
- The Germans dug trenches to defend their captured territory. This led to the establishment of the Western Front and stalemate there until the summer of 1918.

DID YOU KNOW?

The Schlieffen Plan was given that name after the First World War.

To the Germans it was known as 'Aufmarsch I West'. This translates to the 'March West'.

THE TRENCH SYSTEM

'In the front line you could have an ordinary trench, or if the ground was soggy you had, you built barricades of earth and rubble. And trenches could be all sorts of shapes and sizes according to how they'd originally been built and how they'd been knocked about by the enemy' Charles Ward, Middlesex Regiment.

What was the trench system?

Both sides dug networks of trenches to hold their positions on the Western Front. As they were developed they became more sophisticated, and became the soldiers' homes as well as where they fought.

What were the key features of the trench system?

The trenches had 7 key features.

- Frontline trench. This was the first line of defence, and soldiers attacked from here.
- Support trench. This had support troops, and was also a place to retreat to if the front line was attacked and over-run.
- Reserve trench. This was sited 100m behind the support trench. Troops could rest here when they were not on the front line.
- Dugouts. These were holes, dug into the sides of trenches, where men could sleep or take cover.
- Communication trenches. These were used to connect the other trenches together.
- Trenches were cut in a zigzag pattern to stop bullets travelling a long way down them during an attack, or to stop explosions from travelling along the whole trench.
- No man's land. This was the space between the front lines of each side's trenches.

> **DID YOU KNOW?**
>
> The network of trenches was huge, so soldiers needed some way of navigating them.
>
> Names were given to trenches to help with navigation. Sometimes they would have names which related to locations in the UK.

DEADLOCK ON THE WESTERN FRONT

'We're telling lies... we don't tell the public the truth.... that it's impossible to get through on the Western Front.' Lord Rothermere, 1917.

What was deadlock (stalemate) on the Western Front?

The Western Front deadlock, or stalemate, was when both sides dug into their trenches from which they launched repeated attacks, resulting in very little gain and high numbers of casualties.

Why was there a deadlock on the Western Front?

There was deadlock on the Western Front due to a number of factors:

- The failure of the Schlieffen Plan *(p.25)*. As the Germans failed to advance, they dug in at places which were difficult to attack.
- The strength of defences. Trenches were difficult to attack, especially as barbed wire and machine guns were used in defence.
- Ineffective weapons. Attacking weapons struggled against the strong defences early in the war, although weapons developed as the war progressed.
- The conditions. The geography of the Western Front made it difficult to fight. It was difficult to move across ground churned up by shellfire, or turned into muddy quagmires by heavy rain.
- No new tactics. Generals lacked experience in modern, industrialised war. They used old tactics such as cavalry charges and hand-to-hand fighting.

DID YOU KNOW?

One of the biggest myths about the First World War was that most soldiers died.

Only 11.5% of those deployed died. You were actually more likely to die as a British soldier during the Crimean War.

LIFE IN THE TRENCHES

'The cries of the wounded had much diminished now...the reason was only too apparent, for the water was right over the tops of the shell-holes' Captain Edwin Vaughan, 1917

How did people get ill in the First World War trenches?

Living and fighting in the trenches caused soldiers to suffer from a number of illnesses, mainly just from the awful conditions in the trenches.

Why did the trenches make people ill?

The poor conditions, and persistent stress of living in the trenches, led to a number of physical and psychological illnesses.

What common illnesses during the First World War were caused by life in the trenches?

Life in the trenches caused many illnesses, but 5 of the most important were:

- Shell shock *(p.29)*.
- Trench foot *(p.29)*.
- Trench fever *(p.30)*.
- Dysentery *(p.30)*.
- Gangrene. *(p.31)*

DID YOU KNOW?

The biggest killer on the Western Front wasn't from guns or even gas.

It has been estimated that two thirds of casualties during the First World War were actually inflicted by artillery. This makes it by far the biggest killer on the Western Front.

SHELL SHOCK

Every time I went over the top...somebody went insane... but I can see them now coming along, singing you know...absolutely lost their control of everything.' Clifford Lane, Hertfordshire Regiment.

What was shell shock?
The stress of living and fighting in the trenches often caused psychological and mental health problems, known as 'shell shock'.

What were the symptoms of shell shock?
Shell shock could cause nightmares, loss of speech, uncontrollable shaking, and total mental breakdown.

What was the treatment for shell shock?
There was not much understanding about shell shock during the First World War. It was often seen as hysteria, or an attempt to get out of the war.

- Some men who suffered from shell shock were accused of cowardice, and punished.
- Attitudes towards those who suffered from shell shock could be harsh, and they were often accused of cowardice and malingering.
- Electric shock treatments were sometimes used.
- Many shell shock patients were cared for at home or sent to mental asylums.
- 2,000 men were treated for shell shock, including the poets Siegfried Sassoon and Wilfred Owen, at Craiglockhart Hospital in Scotland.

DID YOU KNOW?

Not much was known about the psychological impact of war during the time.

306 British and Commonwealth soldiers were executed for desertion or cowardice during the war. It is now believed that many of these were suffering from shell shock.

TRENCH FOOT

Due to the poor conditions in the trenches, soldiers' feet were extensively exposed to the cold and wet. This lead to a major health concern in the trenches.

What was trench foot?
Standing in cold, wet water led to a condition called trench foot, where the skin was soaked for such long periods of time that it began to rot. It was extremely painful and sometimes led to amputation of the foot.

How was trench foot prevented?
By 1915, the army understood that persistently cold, wet feet led to trench foot. Officials introduced several ways to try and prevent this.

- The feet were rubbed with whale oil to protect them.
- There were regular foot inspections by officers.

TRENCH FEVER

Trenches were infested with lice and other vermin. "The lice were the size of grains of rice, each with its own bite, each with its own itch." Harry Patch.

What was trench fever?
Trench fever affected up to half a million men, causing headaches, high temperatures, and flu-like symptoms.

What caused trench fever?
Rats and lice carried disease through the trenches.

How was trench fever prevented in the First World War?
By 1918, it was discovered that one way trench fever was spread was by lice; this led to the introduction of delousing stations.

> **DID YOU KNOW?**
>
> **Chatting has another meaning!**
> Soldiers would engage in 'chatting' - killing lice on their clothes. An effective method was to run a lighted candle over the places where they laid their eggs.

DYSENTERY

Spread by the unhygienic conditions in the trenches, dysentery was an infection of the intestines which caused extreme diarrhoea.

What caused dysentery in the First World War?
Dysentery spread because of the unhygienic latrines and lack of clean water in the trenches. It caused stomach pains, high temperature, diarrhoea, and even death from dehydration.

How was dysentery prevented in the First World War?
The army began to purify water by adding chloride of lime, but many soldiers didn't like the taste.

> **DID YOU KNOW?**
>
> **Dysentery was one of the biggest causes of illness in the trenches.**
> In one two-month period in 1915, there were 32,528 cases of diarrhoea and dysentery! However, this only led to 231 deaths.

GANGRENE

Another danger of the trenches. With poor hygiene conditions in the trenches, any wound was at risk of developing gas gangrene. Within a couple of days, the wound would swell and gape.

What caused gangrene in the First World War?

Gangrene is the death of body tissue, and occurs when blood supply cannot reach a wound, causing it to rot and produce a foul-smelling gas. It usually affects extremities such as toes, fingers and limbs.

How did they treat gangrene in the First World War?

The only effective treatment for gangrene was amputation of the affected body part, to prevent it spreading and ultimately causing the patient's death.

DID YOU KNOW?

The bacteria which caused gangrene didn't need air to survive!

Clostridia thrived underground. Given the general poor conditions of the trenches, many soldiers were exposed to the bacteria once wounded.

TREATMENT IN THE TRENCHES

The First World War saw the introduction of an effective medical evacuation system. With the increasing casualties, the system had to develop to offer the most effective treatment.

What was the Royal Army Medical Corps?

Doctors and medics in the army belonged to the Royal Army Medical Corps, or RAMC. They worked in different stations on the Western Front.

What was the chain of evacuation for the RAMC?

There was a 'chain of evacuation' to get wounded soldiers to a safe treatment area. The links in the chain were:

- ☑ Regimental Aid Posts (RAP).
- ☑ Dressing stations (ADS and MDS).
- ☑ Casualty Clearing Stations (CCS).
- ☑ Base hospitals.

DID YOU KNOW?

Not all war casualties were men.

Nellie Spindler was a nurse working at a field hospital near Passchendaele. During an artillery attack, Nellie was hit by an exploding shell and died shortly after. She was given a full military funeral.

NEW WEAPONS AND METHODS

Weapons were rapidly advancing alongside technology and modern warfare began to take shape.

What were the main weapons used in the First World War?

There were a number of new weapons and fighting methods introduced during the First World War. These included aircraft *(p.32)*, dogfights, machine guns, poisonous gas, tanks, and artillery.

DID YOU KNOW?

Soldiers were busy underground too!
Both sides employed thousands of miners in special 'tunnelling' units to dig deep mines under each others trenches. Sometimes the mining units would break into each others tunnels and fight fierce battles deep underground.

AIRCRAFT

'The more mechanical become the weapons with which we fight, the less mechanical must be the spirit which controls them' Field Marshal Archibald P Wavell.

What was the role of aircraft in the First World War?

Aircraft were mostly used to gather intelligence on the enemy. This could be in the form of monitoring troop movements, trench layout or supply chains.

What were aircraft like in 1914?

In 1914 aeroplanes were extremely primitive, unarmed, unreliable and highly dangerous 'string bags'. Losses were very high, especially among new pilots.

How did aircraft improve during the war?

By 1918 aircraft were more specialised:

- ☑ 'Fighters' such as the Sopwith Camel were developed. These, were fitted with machine guns and were much faster and more maneuverable. Dogfights were common.
- ☑ 'Bombers', such as the German Gotha and the British Handley Page, had been designed that could carry heavy loads of bombs and drop them on distant targets.
- ☑ By 1918, 10,000 planes were being used and over 50,000 airmen had been killed.

What were dogfights in the First World War?

As aircraft were fitted with machine guns, they could fire on the men in the trenches and also against other enemy planes, in what became known as dogfights. These were spectacular aerial battles relying on a pilot's skill and reflexes.

What impact did aircraft have?

The war sped up the development of aircraft technology so they became a key weapon on the Western Front. Air power was also used at sea to observe and attack shipping.

> **DID YOU KNOW?**
>
> **Zeppelins were more deadly than they looked!**
> Each zeppelin was able to travel at about 85 m.p.h. and carry two tons of bombs.

DOGFIGHTS

'To the aircraft I aim, not the man.' Francesco Baracca

What were dogfights in the First World War?

As aircraft were fitted with machine guns, they could fire on the men in the trenches and also against other enemy planes, in what became known as dogfights. These were spectacular aerial battles relying on a pilot's skill and reflexes.

> **DID YOU KNOW?**
>
> **A pilot who shot done five or more enemy aircraft was called an 'ace'.**
> The most successful ace of the war was Manfred von Richthofen (the Red Baron). He shot down 80 allied planes before being shot down and killed himself in 1918.

MACHINE GUNS

One of the iconic and somewhat overemphasised images of the First World War, machine guns were key to defence.

What was the role of machine guns in the First World War?

Machine guns were used to defend trenches throughout the war. A fairly new weapon, they could fire 400-600 bullets per minute with a range of up to 2,000 metres.

What were machine guns like in 1914?

The Germans had 12,000 in 1914, although the British did not use them in large numbers until 1915. They required a crew of four to six operators so they were more suited to defence than attack. They could rapidly overheat or jam.

How did machine guns improve during the war?

By 1918 they were widely used by all armies. The rate of fire had vastly increased and some handheld 'light machine guns' had been developed e.g. the Lewis gun, so could be used by attacking troops.

What impact did machine guns have?

DID YOU KNOW?

Some things last the test of time...
The British Vickers machine gun was still being used by some armies in the 1960s.

POISON GAS

'They got badly gassed. In the end you could see all these poor chaps laying on the Menin Road, gasping for breath.' Bert Newman, Royal Army Medical Corps.

What was the role of poison gas in the First World War?

The role of gas was to try and help soldiers break into enemy trenches. Gas would cause terror or incapacitate the enemy. It was released from canisters into no-mans-land.

What was poison gas like in 1914?

Poison gas was not used in 1914 but introduced during the battles of 1915:

- Chlorine gas was first used by the Germans at the Second Battle of Ypres in 1915.
- It was released into no-man's land from special canisters hidden in the front line.
- Thousands of French and Canadian soldiers suffocated or fled in terror from the choking green cloud.
- In revenge the British used chlorine gas at the Battle of Loos in September 1915. But winds blew the gas back into the British trenches, gassing more of the attacking troops than the Germans.
- During 1915, all sides began using phosgene and chlorine gas which suffocated and blinded soldiers.

How did poison gas improve during the war?

There were 3 key developments for poison gas during the war:

- By 1917, more lethal gases were developed e.g. mustard gas which burned the skin and lungs.
- Gas shells were introduced and fired at enemy lines to overcome earlier problems of wind direction.
- Specialised gas masks and protective clothing were developed for soldiers, dogs, horses and pigeons, all of whom served in the front lines and were at risk of gas attack.

What impact did poison gas have?

Gas was more of a psychological weapon and did not have a large impact on breaking the stalemate. Gas casualties made up only a small percentage of total casualties as scientists developed effective gas masks. Only 3,000 British troops were killed by gas.

DID YOU KNOW?

'GAS! Quick, boys!—An ecstasy of fumbling.'
The poem 'Dulce et Decorum est' by Wilfred Owen describes a chlorine gas attack and its effects.

TANKS

'Lumbering slowly towards us came three huge mechanical monsters such as we had never seen before.' Bert Chaney, 1916.

What was the role of tanks in the First World War?
Tanks were used to cross difficult ground, destroy machine guns, provide cover for advancing infantry and crush barbed wire in front of enemy trenches. They allowed for quick advancement through the enemy trenches and beyond.

What were tanks like in 1914?
Tanks were used for the first time by the British at the Battle of the Somme *(p.36)* in 1916. They moved at walking pace, were not very manoeuvrable and were extremely unreliable - more than half broke down before they got to the German trenches. The Germans did not use tanks until 1918.

How did tanks improve during the war?
In November 1917 at Cambrai over 400 tanks were used and achieved great success. Unfortunately, they blasted through enemy lines so quickly that the infantry could not keep up.

What impact did tanks have?
Tanks were a key weapon in helping to break the stalemate. They were effective when used in great numbers, something that was only possible in the last year of the war.

DID YOU KNOW?

Tanks were grouped by gender!
The first prototype tank (a male) was named 'Little Willie'. The difference between tank genders was that 'male' tanks were equipped with cannons, while 'female tanks' were equipped with machine guns.

ARTILLERY

Artillery was the weapon of the Western Front, inflicting the most casualties of any weapon.

What was the role of artillery in the First World War?
Artillery was used to bombard the enemy lines by firing huge shells (up to 108 kilograms) in preparation for an infantry attack. The aim was to destroy the barbed wire and the front line trenches which protected the wider trench system.

What was artillery like in 1914?
In 1914 artillery use faced many challenges:

- In 1914 artillery was not very accurate & difficult to 'range' targets by spotting where the shells landed. There was no way for infantry to effectively communicate with the 'gunners' (artillery) from the front line.
- Firing from well behind their own lines, artillery sometimes bombarded their own forward trenches because they could not see where their shells landed.
- By 1915 as many as 50% of British shells were 'duds'.
- Factories could not produce enough shells. The British fired 250,000 shells at the Battle of Loos in 1915 but they

How did artillery improve during the war?

From 1915 major improvements took place in the use of artillery:

- Shells improved in quality and quantity meaning many fewer 'duds'; in 1916 'fuse 106' was developed by the British, which was far more effective at cutting barbed wire.
- Howitzers were improved and more widely used. These fired shells high in the air and so could drop shells into trenches accurately, even if they could not be seen by the gunners.
- New tactics had been introduced e.g. the creeping barrage and the box barrage.
- Spotter aircraft *(p.32)*, spotter balloons and radio were being used to send live information to the artillery about where and what to fire at.

What impact did artillery have?

Artillery bombardments caused more casualties than any other weapon. It was a key weapon of the war.

DID YOU KNOW?

Artillery guns were pretty powerful...
The biggest artillery gun of the war could fire shells weighing over 100kg a distance of 80 miles!

THE BATTLE OF THE SOMME

'The conditions are almost unbelievable. We live in a world of Somme mud. We sleep in it, work in it, fight in it, wade in it and many of us die in it'. Edward Lynch, 1916.

What was the Battle of the Somme?

The Battle of the Somme was fought by British and French forces against the Germans. It was part of an offensive to force the Germans back and achieve victory on the Western Front.

When was the Battle of the Somme?

The battle took place from 1st July, 1916 to 18th November, 1916.

Where was the Battle of the Somme?

It took place on the River Somme in France, where the British and French armies met.

Why was the Somme Offensive launched?

It was part of an offensive to force the Germans back and achieve victory on the Western Front. It was also launched to help relieve pressure on the French, who were under attack at Verdun to the south.

What were the consequences of the Battle of the Somme?

The battle had 4 key outcomes;

- On the first day of the battle there were up to 57,000 British casualties compared with the Germans' 8,000. Haig *(p.38)* continued the attack and, by November, casualties numbered 620,000 for the Allies and 450,000 for the Germans.
- At most, the Allies advanced by 15km along just part of the Western Front. The expected breakthrough never occurred.

- However, the Germans called off their attacks at Verdun, saving the French army there.
- The Allies developed new technology (the tank *(p.35)*) and tactics (the creeping barrage), which contributed to victory later.

Why was the Battle of the Somme unsuccessful?

The battle is seen as an Allied failure for 3 main reasons:

- The Germans knew the attack was coming due to aerial reconnaissance. They moved away from the front line into strengthened trenches, some as deep as 12 metres.
- In the week before the attack, 1.73 million shells were fired at the German lines. However, they were not effective in destroying German dugouts or cutting the barbed wire. Additionally, over a third of those shells fired were 'duds' and failed to explode.
- Following the bombardment of shells, General Haig *(p.38)* told soldiers to advance slowly towards the enemy trenches. He believed they would be undefended; but they were not, and heavy casualties occurred.

> **DID YOU KNOW?**
>
> **The Western Front is still deadly today!**
> Farmers continue to dig up some of the estimated 300 million unexploded shells today. This is known as the 'iron harvest' and, on average, 3 people per year die from coming into contact with unexploded shells.

THE BATTLE OF PASSCHENDAELE

'Perhaps the most hideous fight in the whole war'. George Wrong.

What was the Battle of Passchendaele?

The Battle of Passchendaele was a joint British and Canadian offensive against the Germans, led by General Haig *(p.38)*.

When was the Battle of Passchendaele?

The battle began in July 1917 and finished on 10th November 1917.

Where was the Battle of Passchendaele?

The battle took place in Passchendaele in the Ypres Salient.

What were the aims of the Battle of Passchendaele?

Haig *(p.38)* wanted to break through German lines and control the coast. He wanted to capture naval bases to make it harder for the Germans to carry out submarine attacks on British ships.

What were the results of the Battle of Passchendaele?

There were 3 key outcomes from the battle:

- After three months of fighting, Passchendaele was captured and Haig *(p.38)* could claim victory.
- The battle came at a cost. A total of 240,000 British and 220,000 German soldiers were wounded or killed.
- In total, the Allies captured around 8km of territory, and Haig *(p.38)* failed to achieve his main objective.

Why did the Battle of the Passchendaele fail?

There were 2 main reasons why the battle plan failed:

- As with the Somme *(p.36)*, the Germans were aware of the coming attack.
- Heavy rains turned the battlefield into a quagmire. Soldiers were knee-deep in liquid mud, making it difficult to move.

> **DID YOU KNOW?**
>
> **It was known as the 'Battle of Mud.'**
> With a few days of the battle starting, the area saw the heaviest rainfall since 1884! This completely changed the dynamics of the battle and meant that both sides were well and truly stuck in the mud!

GENERAL HAIG

Haig is one of the more controversial figures of the war. For some, a dynamic leader who engineered new strategies. For others, he is known only as 'the butcher of the Somme'.

Who was General Haig?

General Haig was the British commander on the Western Front from December 1915. He is a controversial figure as some titled him 'Butcher of the Somme *(p.36)*', while others believe he was a key factor in winning the war.

What successes did General Haig have?

General Haig had numerous successes during the First World War:

- Haig relieved the pressure on French forces at Verdun by starting the Somme *(p.36)* Offensive.
- The Battle of Passchendaele *(p.37)* succeeded in weakening the German forces.
- Haig drew German forces away from the Nivelle offensive by leading the Battle of Arras.
- He masterminded victories at Messines in June 1917.
- He was willing to be flexible and experiment with the use of tanks, which had success at Cambrai in 1917.
- He was appointed to win the war for the British, which he ultimately did.

What failures did General Haig have?

Haig had a number of failures during the First World War:

- His tactic of attrition resulted in a huge number of casualties, especially at the battles of the Somme *(p.36)* and Passchendaele *(p.37)*.
- He had a very traditional approach to war, as he was trained as a cavalryman. As such, he was slow to experiment with new methods.
- By 1917, there was still a stalemate. Haig hadn't masterminded an overall victory despite the huge losses.

> **DID YOU KNOW?**
>
> **Haig was one of the key people behind the founding of the Royal British Legion!**
>
> When he returned from the First World War, Haig became the first president of the Royal British Legion. Its aim was to help support those who had served and their families.

THE GERMAN THREAT IN THE NORTH SEA

The war spread to all different theatres and mediums in order to try and gain an advantage. However, the war at sea simply repeated the stalemate of the Western Front.

What was the German naval threat?

Britain had the largest navy in 1914 but, due to the naval arms race, Germany offered a serious challenge. The two navies acted as a mutual deterrent, as both sides wanted to retain their fleets and avoid any major damage. This meant there was also a stalemate at sea for most of the war.

THE BATTLE OF HELIGOLAND

One of the early encounters of the war at sea, this battle set the tone for the remainder of the war in regards to direct ship to ship fighting.

What was the Battle of Heligoland?

The Battle of Heligoland was a British attack on German destroyers in the North Sea.

What happened during the Battle of Heligoland?

A British squadron of 31 destroyers, two cruisers and eight submarines attacked a German patrol.

When was the Battle of Heligoland?

The battle took place on 28th August, 1914.

What were the results of the Battle of Heligoland?

There were 3 key outcomes to the battle;

- ☑ Three German cruisers and one destroyer were sunk, with three more cruisers badly damaged. It also resulted in the death of 712 German sailors, with 530 injured and 336 taken prisoner.
- ☑ Britain suffered damage to one cruiser and three destroyers. 35 sailors were killed with a further 40 injured.
- ☑ The German kaiser was angry at the loss of ships and ordered that any future action must first be approved by him. This meant there was no major fleet action for several months after Heligoland.

> **DID YOU KNOW?**
>
> **The battle was marred by poor vision which led to confusion!**
> Heavy fog, poor communication and poor visibility meant that the battle could have turned out very differently! However, British reinforcements meant that victory was secured.

GERMAN RAIDS

'Come on lad. Let's away downstairs. It's the Germans. Come and look after mother.' Christopher Bennett, 1914.

What were German raids?

The German raids were attacks on British ships and towns.

Why were there German raids on Britain in the First World War?

The German raids had 3 main aims:

- To plant mines that would sink British ships.
- To create an ambush scenario, where British ships would chase German ships nearer to the German coast before being attacked by reinforcements.
- To split up the British fleet into smaller units as they went to defend coastal towns. This would leave the British ships isolated and easier to attack.

When were the German raids?

The Germans carried out two big coastal raids on the English coastline on November 3rd and December 16th, 1914.

Where did the German raids occur?

The Germans bombarded Great Yarmouth in November and then in December they bombarded Scarborough, Whitby and Hartlepool.

What were the results of the German raids?

The Germans were able to lay mines easily at Yarmouth. At Scarborough, shelling took place that destroyed property and killed more than 100 people.

> **DID YOU KNOW?**
>
> **The Germans raid on Hartlepool in December 1914 resulted in the first death on British soil from enemy action for over 200 years!**
> Private Theophilus Jones was just one of the 93 people killed during the raids.

THE BATTLE OF DOGGER BANK

'How was it they got away? What's the explanation? Why didn't you get the lot'. Lord Fisher, 1915.

What was the Battle of Dogger Bank?
The Battle of Dogger Bank was a naval battle in the North Sea between Britain and Germany.

What happened during the Battle of Dogger?
The British learned of an attack in the North Sea and sent a fleet to surprise the Germans. The Germans turned back and the British chased them. The British attacked the fleet, focusing mainly on the German cruiser, Blücher.

When was the Battle of Dogger?
The battle took place on 24th January, 1915.

What were the results of the Battle of Dogger?
The British sank the German cruiser, Blücher, resulting in the deaths of 954 men. Britain didn't lose any ships, although 15 men were killed.

THE BATTLE OF JUTLAND

The largest naval battle of the war and what would become known as the greatest battle of the First World War.

What was the Battle of Jutland?
The Battle of Jutland was the largest naval battle of the First World War, between Britain and Germany off the coast of Denmark.

What happened during the Battle of Jutland?
The Germans intended to draw out the British fleet and make a surprise attack. However, the British already knew of the plan and had sent its fleet ready to attack 259 warships, with 100,000 men on board, fought at Jutland.

When was the Battle of Jutland?
The battle took place between 31st May and 1st June 1916.

What were the results of the Battle of Jutland?
The British suffered the most damage, with 14 ships and 6,000 lives lost. Germany only lost nine ships and 2,500 men. However, both sides claimed victory as, while the Germans had sunk more ships, the German fleet never again left port for fear of being destroyed. Britain continued to control the North Sea.

DID YOU KNOW?

The British were one step ahead!
The Hunstanton coastguard station was able to intercept German transmissions and warn the Admiralty.

SUBMARINE WARFARE

'Even if a submarine should work by a miracle, it will never be used. No country in this world would ever use such a vicious and petty form of warfare!' Admiral William Henderson, 1914.

What was submarine warfare?
Submarine warfare was conducted by the Germans using U-boats to destroy merchant navy ships.

How many ships did Germany sink using submarine warfare?
U-boats were German submarines which were used to sink enemy ships. In 1915, Germany had 21 U-boats and sank 4% of ships supplying Britain, despite the target being to destroy all merchant shipping. By 1917, the number of German U-boats had increased to 200, and they sank 841,114 tonnes of Allied shipping that year.

What tactics did Germany use in U-boat warfare?
The Germans sank all ships entering British waters, regardless of which country they belonged to, until the sinking of the Lusitania *(p.43)* in 1915 almost brought the USA into the war. This was known as unrestricted U-boat warfare. The policy was abandoned until 1917 when an increasingly desperate Germany tried it again, leading the USA to declare war on Germany.

Why did the Germans use submarine warfare?
U-boats were used to destroy merchant ships bringing in food and war materials from abroad. This was in retaliation for the naval blockade of German ports by Britain.

How effective was submarine warfare?
Overall, Germany's U-boat campaign did not have the desired effect:
- Although reduced to six weeks' food supply by 1917, the people of Britain did not starve due to rationing and anti U-boat measures.
- Likewise, the sinking of American ships brought the USA into the war in April 1917.

DID YOU KNOW?

But one step behind in submarine warfare...
The ship, HMS Pathfinder, was the first victim to the German U-boat campaign. Overall, U-boats sunk 13 million tons of merchant goods during the war.

ANTI U-BOAT MEASURES

With such a 'vicious and petty form of warfare', Britain was eager to fight back against the U-boat campaigns.

What were anti U-boat measures?
Britain was in danger of losing the war because the shipping which the country relied on was being sunk by German submarines, or U-boats. Countering the U-boat threat was seen as a very important task.

What anti U-boat measures did the British use in the First World War?

There were 4 main anti U-boat measures brought in by the British to try and avoid the damage being done by German U-boats;

- Minefields were laid across the English Channel and in the North Sea. If a U-boat collided with a mine it would be destroyed.
- Depth charges were introduced. These were explosives which were dropped by the British and exploded at certain depths.
- A convoy system was introduced. This meant merchant ships carrying supplies sailed in groups protected by the Royal Navy.
- Q-ships were introduced. These were warships which looked like merchant ships but they were actually armed and could fight the U-boats.

How successful were British anti U-boat measures?

The anti-U-boat measures were extremely successful for a number of reasons:

- Mines were highly effective. In 1917 alone, 20 out of 63 U-boats were sunk after they collided with mines.
- As crews became more experienced with using depth charges, they became more effective. In 1915 only five U-boats were sunk in this way, but the number reached 22 by 1917.
- Convoys were extremely successful, with only 1% of ships in convoy being destroyed.
- Q-ships attacks accounted for 10% of all U-boats sunk.

DID YOU KNOW?

Things can only get better....

Measures against U-boats improved year upon year. In 1914-15, only 24 were sunk. However, in 1917 alone 65 were sunk.

THE SINKING OF THE LUSITANIA

'The gravity of the situation demands that we should free ourselves from all scruples.' Admiral Friedrich von Ingenohl, 1914.

What happened to the Lusitania?

The Lusitania was a British civilian cruise liner that was sunk by a German U-boat.

When was the Lusitania sunk?

The attack took place on 7th May, 1915.

How was the Lusitania sunk?

The Lusitania departed New York, bound for Liverpool. However, it was torpedoed just 13km from the coast of Ireland by the U20, a German U-boat. The ship sank within 18 minutes.

Who was on the Lusitania?

There were 1,959 passengers on board. Of the 1,198 who drowned, 128 were American.

Why did the Germans sink the Lusitania?

The Germans attacked the Lusitania as there were war materials on board. This made sinking the ship justifiable in the context of war.

What were the reactions to the sinking of the Lusitania?

There was international outrage at the sinking. Britain and America protested and there were calls for America to declare war on Germany. America issued a warning to Germany but did not declare war at that time.

DID YOU KNOW?

The Lusitania still remains in its final resting place.

However, in 2017 divers recovered a telegraph machine from the wreckage and now there are campaigns to raise the ship. There is some urgency to this because bacteria is currently eating away at the wreckage and eventually, there will be nothing of the ship left.

THE GALLIPOLI CAMPAIGN

An attempt to control the Dardanelles and defeat the Ottoman Empire ended in disaster and humiliation. Churchill would live with the failed campaign on his record for the rest of his political life.

What was the Gallipoli campaign?

The campaign was an Allied attempt to open up another campaign and to draw German forces away from the Western front.

What were the aims of the Gallipoli campaign?

In October 1914, Turkey joined forces with Germany and Austria-Hungary. As Turkey controlled the Dardanelles, which connected the Mediterranean Sea to the Black Sea, Britain could no longer send supplies to Russia, and Russian ships in the Black Sea were trapped. The Gallipoli campaign was needed to:

- Supply Russia through the Black Sea ports.
- Break the stalemate on the Western Front by drawing in German forces to support its weaker ally, Turkey.

Who was in charge of the Gallipoli campaign?

It was an Anglo-French operation led by Winston Churchill, the British first lord of the Admiralty.

When was the Gallipoli campaign?

The campaign ran from February 1915 to January 1916.

Where was the Gallipoli campaign?

At Gallipoli, in northwest Turkey.

What happened during the Gallipoli campaign?

There were a number of events during the Gallipoli campaign:

- On 19th February, 1915, Anglo-French naval forces began to bombard Turkish positions along the coast. 18th March, 1915 saw the main attack launched, but the fleet retreated after losing three battleships.
- After the retreat, the decision was taken to launch a ground invasion. Allied troops landed on 25th April, 1915, with the aim of capturing the forts that guarded the entrance to the Dardanelles.
- The naval attack warned the Turks of the planned invasion, so they were prepared and had strengthened their positions since February 1915.
- Allied troops landed at Anzac Cove under heavy fire, but established themselves. However, they were unable to move inland and a stalemate developed.
- The Allies withdrew between 10th December, 1915 and 9th January, 1916. Over 135,000 Allied troops were evacuated. This was the most successful part of the campaign, with only three casualties recorded.

What were the results of the Gallipoli campaign?

There were 5 important consequences of the failed campaign:

- 204,000 Allied troops were wounded and 48,000 killed.
- Many soldiers became ill, due to the poor living conditions.
- The Dardanelles were not captured, and this meant Russia was cut off from Allied support.
- Germany was able to strengthen its Western Front position as the Allies looked to make gains in Gallipoli.
- Churchill and Hamilton (the leaders of the campaign) were removed from their positions.

DID YOU KNOW?

Gallipoli nearly ruined Winston Churchill's political career!

Even years after the campaign, speeches by Churchill would be heckled with, 'What about the Dardanelles?'

THE LUDENDORFF OFFENSIVE

Germany's last gamble with Ludendorff stating "we must strike at the earliest moment before the Americans can throw strong forces into the scale. We must beat the British."

What was the Ludendorff Offensive?

The Ludendorff Offensive, also known as the 1918 Spring Offensive or Kaiserschlacht, was a series of German attacks along the Western Front.

Why was the Ludendorff Offensive launched?

The offensive was launched by Germany for a number of reasons:

- The USA was sending 50,000 troops each month to the Western Front, along with vast amounts of weapons and equipment.
- The withdrawal of Russia freed up hundreds of thousands of troops from the Eastern Front.
- By 1918 the British naval blockade meant Germany was running out of food and war materials.

Who planned the Ludendorff Offensive?

Erich Ludendorff, a German general, planned the campaign.

When did the Ludendorff Offensive happen?

The offensive was launched on 21st March 1918 and ended in July 1918.

What happened during the Ludendorff Offensive?

The Ludendorff Offensive was a series of key events:

- On 21st March, 600 German guns began a five-hour bombardment of enemy trenches. This was followed by the release of mustard gas.
- Specially trained and lightly armed stormtroopers then advanced towards the enemy trenches, moving quickly and bypassing strong defences.
- As the British retreated, tens of thousands were captured and the Germans continued to advance.
- 100,000 German infantry soldiers then followed and this strategy allowing the Germans to capture 65km of French territory by July.
- At the Second Battle of the Marne, 20,000 US troops arrived to reinforce the Allies. This halted the German attack.

Why did the Ludendorff Offensive fail?

The offensive failed for a number of reasons:

- Ludendorff sent too many men into France. He did not have any reserves or replacement troops.
- The offensive moved too quickly. The supply chain couldn't keep up and soldiers ran out of food and ammunition.
- The attack created a salient in the German line, which could be attacked from three sides. This meant the Germans were vulnerable to counter-attacks which could break their line.
- Hungry German soldiers stopped to loot food and wine from captured villages and Allied supply dumps, slowing the advance.

DID YOU KNOW?

The Ludendorff Offensive was also known by another name!

Kaiserschlacht (translated to Kaiser's Battle) was another name given to the offensive. It is also sometimes referred to as the Spring Offensive...as if there weren't enough First World War battles and names to remember!

THE USA AND ITS ENTRY TO THE FIRST WORLD WAR

Following years of neutrality, a number of key events sparked Woodrow Wilson to ask Congress for a declaration of war. They agreed and on 6th April 1917, they joined forces with the Allies.

What did the USA do when it joined the First World War?

When the USA joined the First World War it reinforced the Allies in Europe, and helped by continuing to supply other allies with food, arms, money, and raw materials.

When did the USA join the First World War?

The USA formally declared war in April 1917.

Why did the USA enter the First World War?

The USA joined the First World War for two key reasons:

- ☑ The 'Zimmerman Telegram', from the German foreign secretary to the German ambassador in Mexico, was leaked in January 1917. It offered military and financial support if Mexico agreed to invade the USA. While the Mexicans did not agree, this created tension between Germany and the USA.
- ☑ Germany had restarted its unrestricted U-boat campaign. This resulted in the sinking of five American ships in March 1917. As the USA had warned Germany against this after the sinking of the Lusitania *(p.43)*, it felt it had no choice but to declare war on Germany.

When did American troops arrive in Europe after they entered the First World War?

The first American troops landed in Europe in June 1917.

How did America's entry into the First World War help the Allies?

America's entry into the First World War helped in 4 key ways:

- ☑ By May 1918 there were over one million US troops in France with tens of thousands arriving each week.
- ☑ They enlarged French ports so arriving ships could deliver more men and supplies.
- ☑ They built over 1,600km of railway lines to help continue the supply chain.
- ☑ They laid over 16,000km of telephone and telegraph cables, to help improve communications between lines.

Why was US entry into the First World War important?

There were a number of significant events in which the USA was involved:

- ☑ In the Second Battle of the Marne, two divisions of American soldiers helped to prevent German forces taking Paris during the Ludendorff Offensive *(p.45)*.
- ☑ In the Second Battle of Albert, in August 1918, 108,000 US soldiers helped capture 8,000 German soldiers.
- ☑ On 12th September 1918, in the Saint-Mihiel Offensive, 500,000 US soldiers attacked the salient created during the Ludendorff Offensive *(p.45)*. Within four days, the salient was under Allied control.
- ☑ Between 26th September and 11th November 1918, the US led a combined US-Franco force of more than one million men. Using 300 tanks and 500 US aircraft *(p.32)*, the force advanced 32km towards the German border.
- ☑ The US was able to supply the Allies with large numbers of tanks and artillery.

DID YOU KNOW?

Once the Americans had joined the war, they became increasingly paranoid about German influences in the US!

German names such for items such as frankfurters, sauerkraut and dachshunds were all changed. These were replaced with more American names such as Liberty Sausage.

THE HUNDRED DAYS OFFENSIVE

Germany in retreat. Following the first day of defeats, Ludendorff referred to 8th August 1918 as 'the Black Day of the German Army'. This was the beginning of the end.

What was the 100 Days Offensive?

The 100 Days Offensive was a series of Allied attacks which ended the First World War.

What happened during the 100 Days Offensive?

There were 2 key events of the 100 Days Offensive:

- ☑ At Amiens an artillery attack and creeping barrage broke through the German lines and allowed an Allied advance of 25km. Allied troops also captured 48,000 German soldiers.
- ☑ After breaking the front line at Amiens, the Allies forced the Germans back to the Hindenburg Line which was broken by 8th October. At this point, the Germans were now in all-out retreat.

When was the 100 Days Offensive?

The offensive began with the Battle of Amiens on 8th August 1918, and ended officially on 11th November 1918 when Germany signed the Armistice.

Why was the 100 Days Offensive important?

The 100 Days Offensive was important for 2 key reasons:

- ☑ It allowed the Allies to break the Hindenburg Line, a defensive line of three trench systems. Once this was broken, the Germans retreated in huge numbers.
- ☑ The offensive led to the German High Command seeking an armistice which came into effect on 11th November, 1918

DID YOU KNOW?

The 100 day offensive wasn't actually 100 days...
It only lasted 95 days from 8th August 1918 to 11th November 1918.

THE END OF THE FIRST WORLD WAR

Following the failure of the Ludendorff Offensive and the success of the Allies' 100 Days Offensive, Germany was left facing a humiliating defeat.

Was Germany defeated in the First World War?

Germany requested an armistice, and this was signed between Germany and the Allies on 11th November 1918. This was the formal end to the fighting while a peace treaty was negotiated.

What were the reasons for the German defeat in the First World War?

There were a number of reasons for Germany's overall defeat in the First World War:

- ☑ Food and famine. Germany's agricultural production was poor and it relied on foreign imports. However, the British naval blockade starved Germany of these, and there was a series of bad harvests. As the Germans starved, they rioted against the government.
- ☑ Political turmoil. There was a series of riots and revolts against the government. In October there was a naval mutiny followed by revolutions in Munich and, finally, riots in Berlin. This caused the kaiser to abdicate.
- ☑ Military defeat. Germany realised it was facing a military defeat. With the failure of the Ludendorff Offensive *(p.45)*, the introduction of two million US troops and its allies surrendering, Germany knew it could no longer continue the fight.

> **DID YOU KNOW?**
>
> **The armistice was signed at 5am in a railway carriage in Compiegne, France.**
>
> This event proved significant enough for Hitler to use the same carriage to accept the French surrender during the Second World War.

GLOSSARY

A

Abdicate - to give up a position of power or a responsibility.

Agricultural - relating to agriculture.

Alliance - a union between groups or countries that benefits each member.

Allies - parties working together for a common objective, such as countries involved in a war. In both world wars, 'Allies' refers to those countries on the side of Great Britain.

Ambassador - someone, often a diplomat, who represents their state, country or organisation in a different setting or place.

Ammunition - collective term given to bullets and shells.

Amputate, Amputation - to surgically remove a limb from someone's body.

Annex, Annexation, Annexed - to forcibly acquire territory and add it to a larger country.

Armistice - an agreement between two or more opposing sides in a war to stop fighting.

Artillery - large guns used in warfare.

Assassinate - to murder someone, usually an important figure, often for religious or political reasons.

Assassination - the act of murdering someone, usually an important person.

Attrition - the act of wearing down an enemy until they collapse through continued attacks.

B

Blockade - a way of blocking or sealing an area to prevent goods, supplies or people from entering or leaving. It often refers to blocking transport routes.

Box barrage - The firing shells at the enemy on three sides to prevent them retreating or sending reinforcements into a battle.

C

Campaign - a political movement to get something changed; in military terms, it refers to a series of operations to achieve a goal.

Casualties - people who have been injured or killed, such as during a war, accident or catastrophe.

Cavalry - the name given to soldiers who fight on horseback.

Central Powers - Germany and its allies during the First World War.

Civilian - a non-military person.

Coalition, Coalitions - a temporary alliance, such as when a group of countries fights together.

Colonies, Colony - a country or area controlled by another country and occupied by settlers.

Convoy - a group of ships or vehicles travelling together, usually protected by armed troops.

Counter-attack - an attack made in response to one by an opponent.

Creeping barrage - a slowly advancing artillery bombardment which attacking troops can follow for protection.

D

Deadlock - a situation where no action can be taken and neither side can make progress against the other; effectively a draw.

Deterrent - something that discourages an action or behaviour.

Dreadnought - A battleship, which was more powerful in firepower and defence than prior models.

Dud - a bomb, shell or mine that fails to explode.

E

Economic - relating to the economy; also used when justifying something in terms of profitability.

Empire - a group of states or countries ruled over and controlled by a single monarch.

Encircle, Encirclement - a military term for enemy forces isolating and surrounding their target.

F

Famine - a severe food shortage resulting in starvation and death, usually the result of bad harvests.

Fasting - to deliberately refrain from eating, and often drinking, for a period of time.

Free trade - the policy of trading between countries without any taxes, with the aim of increasing trade links.

Front - in war, the area where fighting is taking place.

G

Gangrene - the death of body tissue due to either lack of blood or serious bacterial infection.

H

Heir - someone who is entitled to property or rank following the current owner or holder's death.

I

Imperial, Imperialisation, Imperialism, Imperialist - is the practice or policy of taking possession of, and extending political and economic control over other areas or territories. Imperialism always requires the use of military, political or economic power by a stronger nation over that of a weaker one. An imperialist is someone who supports or practices imperialism and imperial relates to a system of empire, for example the British Empire.

Import - to bring goods or services into a different country to sell.

GLOSSARY

Independence, Independent - to be free of control, often meaning by another country, allowing the people of a nation the ability to govern themselves.

Industrial - related to industry, manufacturing and/or production.

Industrialisation, Industrialise, Industrialised - the process of developing industry in a country or region where previously there was little or none.

Infantry - soldiers who march and fight on foot.

K

Kaiser - the German word for a king or emperor.

L

Limb - an arm or leg.

Lord, Lords - a man of high status, wealth and authority.

M

Mandate - authority to carry out a policy.

Medic - someone who has medical knowledge but is not a doctor.

Merchant ships - unarmed ships used for carrying supplies and goods.

Mine - an explosive device usually hidden underground or underwater.

Mobilisation - the action of a country getting ready for war by preparing and organising its armed forces.

Morass - an area of swampy or very wet and muddy ground which is difficult to cross.

Mutiny - a rebellion or revolt, in particular by soldiers or sailors against their commanding officers.

N

Nationalism, Nationalist, Nationalistic - identifying with your own nation and supporting its interests, often to the detriment or exclusion of other nations.

Naval supremacy - when a navy is that strong, enemies are unable to attack; sometimes referred to as command of the sea.

No man's land - the land between the opposing sides' trenches in the First World War.

O

Offensive - another way of saying an attack or campaign.

P

Psychological - referring to a person's mental or emotional state.

Q

Quagmire - an area of swampy or very wet and muddy ground which is difficult to cross.

R

Raid - a quick surprise attack on the enemy.

Rationing - limiting goods that are in high demand and short supply.

Rebels - people who rise in opposition or armed resistance against an established government or leader.

Reconnaissance - observation of an enemy in order to gain useful information such as its position, strategy or capabilities.

Revolution - the forced overthrow of a government or social system by its own people.

Riots - violent disturbances involving a crowd of people.

Rolling barrage - a slowly advancing artillery bombardment which attacking troops can follow for protection.

S

Sabotage - to deliberately destroy, damage or obstruct, especially to gain a political or military advantage.

Salient - in military terms, a piece of land that protrudes into enemy territory; also known as a bulge.

Stalemate - a situation where no action can be taken and neither side can make progress against the other; effectively a draw.

Strategy - a plan of action outlining how a goal will be achieved.

Symptom - an indication of something, such as a sign of a particular illness.

T

Tactic - a strategy or method of achieving a goal.

Territories, Territory - an area of land under the control of a ruler/country.

Treaty - a formal agreement, signed and ratified by two or more parties.

U

U-boat - the German name for a submarine.

Ultimatum - a final demand, with the threat of consequences if it is not met.

W

Weltpolitik - Germany's pre-First World War foreign policy which aimed to turn Germany into a global power by acquiring overseas colonies and developing its navy.

INDEX

A
Aircraft - 32
Alliances - 15
Allied 100 Days - 47
Anti U-boat measures - 42
Artillery - 35
Assassination, Archduke Franz Ferdinand - 24

B
Balkan War, First - 22
Balkan War, Second - 22
Battle of Dogger - 41
Battle of Heligoland - 39
Battle of Jutland - 41
Battle of Passchendaele - 37
Battle of the Somme - 36
Black Hand - 23
Bosnian Crisis - 21
Britain, German raids on - 40

D
Deadlock, Western Front - 27
Dogger, Battle of - 41
Dreadnought - 18
Dysentery - 30

E
Economic rivalry - 16

F
First Balkan War - 22
First Moroccan Crisis - 19
First World War - 14
Franz Ferdinand, assassination - 24

G
Gallipoli campaign - 44
Gangrene - 31
Germany, defeat - 48
Germany, naval threat - 39
Germany, raids on Britain - 40

H
Haig, General Douglas - 38
Heligoland, Battle of - 39

I
Illness, WW1 trenches - 28
Imperialism - 15

J
July Days (July Crisis), 1914 - 25
Jutland, Battle of - 41

K
Kaiserschlacht - 45

L
Ludendorff Offensive - 45
Lusitania, sinking of - 43

M
Machine guns - 33
Militarism - 14
Moroccan Crisis, 1905 - 19
Moroccan Crisis, 1911 - 20

N
Nationalism - 16
Naval Race - 18

O
One Hundred Day Offensive - 47

P
Passchendaele, Battle of - 37
Poison gas - 34

R
RAMC - 31
Royal Army Medical Corps - 31

S
Schlieffen Plan - 25
Second Balkan War - 22
Second Moroccan Crisis - 20
Shell shock - 29

INDEX

Somme, Battle of - 36
Spring Offensive - 45
Stalemate, Western Front - 27
Submarine warfare - 42

T

Tanks - 35
Trench fever - 30
Trench foot - 29
Trench system - 26
Triple Alliance - 17
Triple Entente - 18

U

U-boat warfare - 42
USA, entry to WW1 - 46

W

Weapons - 32
    Aircraft - 32
    Artillery - 35
    Machine guns - 33
    Poison gas - 34
    Tanks - 35
Western Front, deadlock - 27

Milton Keynes UK
Ingram Content Group UK Ltd.
UKHW051838291223
435200UK00006B/82